Protecting Our Planet

What Can We Do About INVASIVE SPECIES?

Lorijo Metz

PowerKiDS press

New York

To Julie Hamilton and Vicky Fitzmaurice, the gardeners of St. Francis

Published in 2010 by The Rosen Publishing Group, Inc.
29 East 21st Street, New York, NY 10010

First Edition

Editor: Amelie von Zumbusch
Book Design: Kate Laczynski
Photo Researcher: Jessica Gerweck

Photo Credits: Cover, p. 1 © Michael & Patricia Fogden/Corbis; pp. 4, 8, 12, 16, 20 Shutterstock.com ; p. 6 Roy Toft/Getty Images; p. 10 Reinhard Dirscherl/Getty Images; p. 14 Melissa Farlow/Getty Images; p. 18 © Reuters/Corbis.

Library of Congress Cataloging-in-Publication Data

Metz, Lorijo.
  What can we do about invasive species? / Lorijo Metz. — 1st ed.
     p. cm. — (Protecting our planet)
  Includes index.
  ISBN 978-1-4042-8084-7 (library binding) — ISBN 978-1-4358-2487-4 (pbk.) — ISBN 978-1-4358-2488-1 (6-pack)
  1. Biological invasions. 2. Biological invasions.—Control. 3. Nonindigenous pests. 4. Nonindigenous pests.—Control. I. Title.
  QH353.M48 2010
  577'.18—dc22

                                    2008055828

Manufactured in China

CONTENTS

People brought camels to Australia, where they became an invasive species. Camels eat native plants. Camels also use food that native animals need.

Invasive Species

Our Earth is home to many wonderful plants and animals. These living things and the **environment** in which they live make up ecosystems. Plants and animals that have lived in an ecosystem for a long time are native species. Native species **depend** on each other and **protect** the environment in which they live. Sometimes, new species invade, or enter, ecosystems. These invasive species multiply so quickly that they crowd out native species.

People often spread invasive species without knowing it. Rats, an invasive species from India, spread far and wide by creeping onto ships. Rats destroy birds and plants all over the world.

The Perfect Niche

Within an ecosystem, every living thing has a niche, or a place. For example, in a pond ecosystem, big fish eat little fish. Little fish often eat bugs or plants. Plants clean the water. Everything works well together, and there is enough food for all.

An ecosystem can change a lot if one invasive species, such as the water hyacinth plant, moves in. Water hyacinths multiply quickly and, if not controlled, cover ponds. This blocks the sun, which kills plants and the fish that eat them. With fewer fish, bugs, such as mosquitoes, multiply out of control.

Plants Running Wild

Invasive plants are sometimes called weeds. They often produce many seeds and can grow in several environments. These plants spread quickly, taking water and sunlight from native plants. While the wind and birds carry invasive seeds far from home, so do humans.

People brought the Japanese kudzu vine to America because they thought it was beautiful. Horses and cows also love to eat it. However, kudzu vines grow up to 1 foot (.3 m) per day and quickly kill plants and trees in their paths. Today, the American government spends large amounts of money trying to control this plant.

DID YOU KNOW?

Cheatgrass, which is native to Europe and Asia, is a problem in North America. This grass dries out easily. In California, cheatgrass feeds fires that break out in dry weather.

The Northern pike is an invasive fish in several American states, such as Florida, Alaska, Maine, and Colorado.

Troublesome Insects and Fish

Invasive **insects** may be tiny, but they are big trouble. For example, red imported fire ants have a painful bite that can kill humans and cows. These powerful ants came by ship from South America to North America. Asian tiger mosquitoes traveled to America in used tires. They can carry West Nile virus, an illness that can be deadly to humans.

The snakehead fish is an invasive species from China. It is a problem in the Potomac River near Washington, D.C. These fish can breathe air as they wiggle over land between bodies of water. Snakehead fish eat other fish and quickly destroy native species.

DID YOU KNOW?

The balsam woolly adelgid, which comes from Europe, is an invasive species in North America. This tiny bug eats fir trees, including the balsam firs often used for Christmas trees.

People who wanted to raise nutrias for their fur brought them from South America to the United States. Today, nutrias are an invasive species.

Some Common Invaders

You might be surprised to learn that the European rabbit is an invasive **mammal**. In 1859, 24 rabbits were let go into the wilds of Australia. Since they had few natural **predators** there, the number of rabbits grew quickly. By 1926, Australia had about 10 **billion** rabbits. They hurt the soil by eating too many plants. The rabbits also took food from native mammals.

Common pigeons also multiply quickly. These invasive birds are a problem in many places, from the United States to the Galápagos Islands. Pigeons may carry illnesses that make humans, native birds, and other animals sick. These birds eat farmers' crops, too.

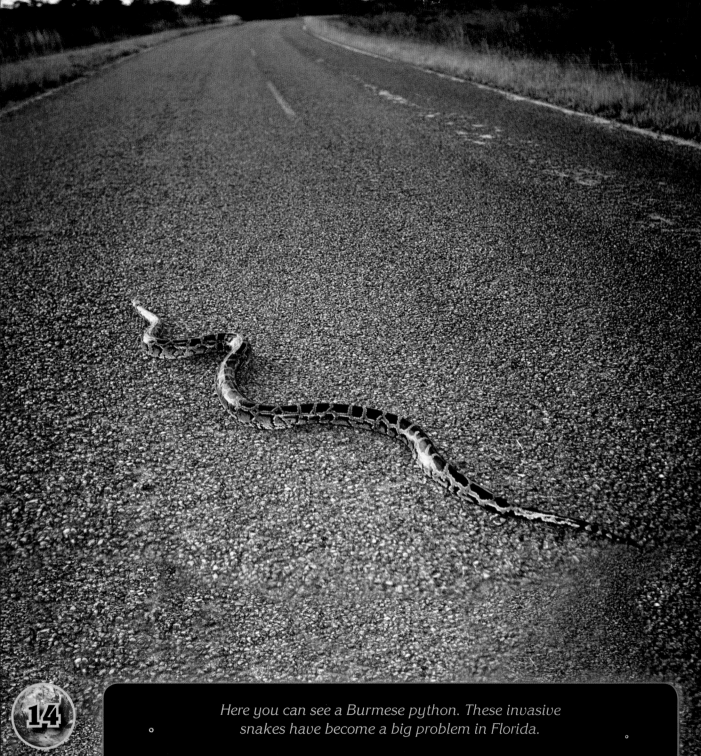

Here you can see a Burmese python. These invasive snakes have become a big problem in Florida.

When Pets Become Invasive Species

Pets can become an invasive species when they escape or are let go by their owners. In the wild, dogs and cats must eat native plants and animals to live. These common pets have destroyed ecosystems.

Exotic pets, like the Burmese python, are often let go when they become too large or too much work for their owners. The Florida Everglades is overrun with hungry Burmese pythons. These powerful snakes can grow to be up to 20 feet (6 m) long. The snakes feed on native animals. Burmese pythons even eat **endangered** animals, such as the mangrove fox squirrel.

DID YOU KNOW?

Though they were once common exotic pets, African land snails are now against the law to sell in the United States. These snails can spread deadly illnesses to humans.

Indian mynah birds are an invasive species in Hawaii. They eat native plants and help spread an invasive plant, called lantana.

Invading Islands

Invasive species are an especially big problem on islands. Over time, island species change to fit their ecosystem niches exactly. However, these species often change in ways that make it easy for new species to destroy them.

Brown tree snakes arrived on the island of Guam in the 1950s. With no natural predators, the snakes multiplied quickly and killed many native birds, lizards, and other small animals. On Tahiti and Hawaii, native forests have been taken over by flowering velvet trees, from South America. These trees' large leaves block sunlight, which lets no plants grow under them. This causes soil **erosion** on hillsides.

How to Deal with Invasive Species

People use several methods to control invasive species. One method is to place predators in ecosystems to kill or slow the growth of invasive species. This is known as biocontrol. **Chemicals** are also used to kill or drive out invasive species. However, both these methods may hurt other living things as well as invasive species.

Live **capture** is a way of controlling invasive species that avoids hurting nearby native species. This method means removing invasive species without killing them. Invasive plants and animals that have been removed may be returned to their native ecosystems or placed in a controlled environment.

DID YOU KNOW?

Zebra mussels are invasive shellfish that cover boats and get into pipes. Hot water, hot air, chemicals, and even sound are some of the methods people use to control these mussels.

Caring for Native Species

In a healthy ecosystem, plants, animals, and nonliving things work well together. Everything has its own niche. After an invasive species is removed from an ecosystem, it is important to bring back the native species that it has driven out.

Caring for native species protects biodiversity. Biodiversity is having a lot of different types of species living together in an ecosystem. Invasive species take away biodiversity. This can make nonliving things, such as soil and water, less healthy. Planting and **promoting** native species is important because the living and nonliving parts of the ecosystem take care of each other.

What Can We Do?

Learning about invasive species is an important step toward protecting native species. Before adding a new plant to your garden, make sure it is not an invasive species. You can also become a member of a community group that removes invasive species or plants native ones.

If you can no longer care for your pet, ask your librarian for a list of places that would take it. Think carefully before buying an exotic pet. Some exotic pets, such as Burmese pythons, need special cages so that they will not escape. There are many ways you can help protect Earth's biodiversity!

GLOSSARY

billion (BIL-yun) One thousand million.

capture (KAP-chur) Taking control of something by force.

chemicals (KEH-mih-kulz) Matter that can be mixed with other matter to cause changes.

depend (dih-PEND) To count on someone or something.

endangered (in-DAYN-jerd) In danger of no longer living.

environment (en-VY-ern-ment) All the natural things in a place.

erosion (ih-ROH-zhun) The wearing away of land over time.

exotic (ek-ZAH-tik) Strange, or from a far-off place.

insects (IN-sekts) Small animals that often have six legs and wings.

mammal (MA-mul) A warm-blooded animal that has a backbone and hair, breathes air, and feeds milk to its young.

predators (PREH-duh-terz) Animals that kill other animals for food.

promoting (pruh-MOHT-ing) Raising attention about something.

protect (pruh-TEKT) To keep safe.

INDEX

WEB SITES

Due to the changing nature of Internet links, PowerKids Press has developed an online list of Web sites related to the subject of this book. This site is updated regularly. Please use this link to access the list: www.powerkidslinks.com/ourpl/species/